I C O N S
OF AUSTRALIA

Steve Parish

THE SIGNATURE COLLECTION

Previous page: The Flinders Ranges, around 450 km north of Adelaide, South Australia, are known for their rugged beauty and the colour changes they undergo as the day progresses.

Sydney Harbour Bridge, opened in 1932, joins the city centre to the north shore of Sydney Harbour. It is recognised world wide as a symbol of Australia's largest city.

Sunshine, sand, surf and the sea — the scene that Australians regard as a birthright and overseas visitors enjoy to the full.

CONTENTS

INTRODUCTION

Australia itself is an icon to some people, one that represents independence, resourcefulness, and enduring spirit. In part, this is due to the nature of the continent: the vast distances, the variances in temperatures and rainfall, the landforms, waterways and surrounding oceans, the vegetation and wildlife. And, in turn, this depth of feeling for natural Australia contributes to the human environment: the architecture, the towns and cities, the harnessing of natural resources, the people and their lifestyles that are today's multicultural Australia.

From its very beginning as part of the supercontinent, Gondwana, Australia's coastlines and oceans have enclosed remarkable and unique plants and creatures. Its isolation from other landmasses has resulted in remnants of those far-off days being preserved, either living or fossilised. Today's Australia is the result of human interaction with the natural world, and today's Australians and other global villagers must be mindful of the fragility of the very special place we share.

I strongly feel that there is much about this country that is iconic in the modern world. To convey this, I have chosen to portray the country's strengths — those elements of Australia that are icons for what we value and what we can achieve. There are landscapes that are so powerful that their image and aura stay in the mind forever. Some of them, such as the awesome monolith, Uluru, are international icons, as are such architectural gems as the Sydney Opera House and the Sydney Harbour Bridge. Some Australian icons are of significance nationally, locally or personally.

Share with me images that have such meaning for me that they are icons for the power and beauty of Nature or for human ingenuity and endeavour.

Steve Parish

Opposite: The great red rock Uluru is an object of pilgrimage for sightseers, nature lovers, photographers and adventurers. It stands in the south-west of the Northern Territory.

NEW SOUTH WALES

THE PREMIER STATE

First of the Australian States to be established, New South Wales is centred on the continent's most famous and populous city, Sydney. That capital is home to several of Australia's most notable constructions — Sydney Harbour Bridge, Sydney Opera House, Sydney Tower, Circular Quay, the Olympic complex at Homebush Bay, Sydney Cricket Ground and Darling Harbour are just a few. The city is built around Sydney Harbour, an icon in itself.

West from Sydney lie the scenic splendours of the Blue Mountains, with landmarks such as the Three Sisters and Govetts Leap. Further west stretch vast plainlands, where the image of the Outback, with its ringers, shearers and drovers, was born. Still further west the deserts, dotted with mining towns that contribute minerals and precious stones to the continent's coffers, stretch to the horizon. South and north of Sydney, golden beaches lie between coastal resorts; the Great Dividing Range stretches from Queensland to the Victorian borders, cloaked in rainforests in the north, capped with winter snows in the south.

New South Wales is rich in traditions — a place where icons originate.

Opposite: An aerial view of central Sydney, capital city of New South Wales.

Above: The Breadknife, a volcanic formation in the Warrumbungle Mountains.

An aerial shot over Sydney's splendid Harbour, spanned by the Harbour Bridge and enhanced by the Opera House, portrays the spirit of this great city.

Sydney is fortunate enough to have sedate, peaceful Harbour beaches and also to be within easy reach of a chain of golden ocean beaches, blessed with the crystalline waves of the Pacific Ocean. It was on these beaches, back in the early 1900s, that the surf lifesaving movement was born and the image of the bronzed Aussie lifesaver was fixed for the world's appreciation. Today's lifesavers are volunteers who carry out rescues and also stage immensely popular carnivals, showcasing traditional and modern lifesaving methods and surf skills.

Sydney is not the only Australian city to have easy access to magnificent beaches: Canberra is the only landlocked capital, and each of the others is within reach of beaches as brilliant as Sydney's favourites: Bondi, Manly, Coogee and Maroubra.

A view across Manly Ocean Beach and Manly Cove to North Harbour.

*Bondi is the closest ocean beach to Sydney city. Once called "Bundi", it has become
synonymous with Australia's beach culture: a place to swim, surf, see and be seen.*

The Blue Mountains rise just west of Sydney. Their most notable features include the famous

Three Sisters and the Jamison Valley, both of which may be viewed from a cable car.

ALL TYPES OF MOUNTAINS

The Great Dividing Range runs the length of the New South Wales, to the west of the State's fertile coastal plain. It abounds in dramatic scenery, forested gorges, swift rivers and waterfalls and the southern section is snow-covered in wintertime. One of the most scenic sections, the Blue Mountains, offers spectacular sandstone cliffs and wild valleys. Only 65 km west of Sydney, that city's residents have been taking summer refuge in the cooler heights for over a century. Northern New South Wales's highland wonders include the World Heritage wildernesses of Dorrigo and New England National Parks, as well as the ancient volcanic remnants known as Mount Warning, Mount Kaputar and the Warrumbungles. To Sydney's south, the Great Divide reaches a climax in the Australian Alps, high alpine terrain that includes Morton and Kosciuszko National Parks.

In the south-east of New South Wales, the high points of the Great Dividing Range are snow-covered in winter. The Australian Alps offer snow sports as fine as any in the world.

The end of a perfect summer day on Lord Howe Island, off the coast of New South Wales and two hours' flight from Sydney. In the background are Mt Lidgbird and Mt Gower.

CONQUERING COASTS

A beach is a sandy, inviting place to swim, sunbake and surf.

A coast is a whole lot more. A coast has sandy beaches, certainly, but it also has rocky headlands, precipitous cliffs, offshore islands, wavecut platforms, river estuaries, mangrove swamps, underwater reefs and many other features. A coast is a place for adventures — serious fishing, scrambling over rocks, peering into pools for crabs and anemones and fishes left behind by the retreating tide — or a place for reflection — sitting on a headland watching ships, seabirds and migrating whales go past.

The New South Wales coastline offers opportunities for all these pleasures. From the pelican-haunted estuaries of the northern rivers to the safe harbour of Twofold Bay and beyond to the Victorian border, this coast is paradise for locals and holiday-makers alike.

One of New South Wales' magnificent northern beaches. This one is lapped by the waters of Byron Bay and overlooked by Cape Byron, most easterly point on the mainland of Australia.

Methods of removing the woolly fleeces of sheep change with the passage of time, but the sheep and the shearers themselves are the stuff of Australian folklore.

AUSSIE LEGENDS

On the western side of the Great Divide, annual rainfall decreases dramatically. Towns, farms and pastoral properties draw water from the network of creeks and rivers that drain into the Murrumbidgee, the Darling and eventually reach the mighty Murray river. Stock and wildlife drink at bores dispensing water from the ancient reservoirs of the Great Artesian Basin. Further west still is country which comes to life only after heavy rainfall, when hardy plants hasten through budding and blossoming to set seeds to survive the next dry spell.

This is the country of Australian legend, of ringers and gun shearers, of feats of daring when bushfires ravage the plains, or floods overwhelm flocks and herds, and of endurance when drought sucks the life from the land. This is the country of the Eleventh Commandment — never let your mate down.

Cattle graze on the vast plainlands west of the Great Dividing Range.

The hotel at Silverton, near Broken Hill in the south-west of New South Wales. Once a roaring mining town, Silverton has become a favourite haunt of artists and film crews.

THE PAST PRESERVED

Eastern Australia was claimed for Great Britain in 1770 by Captain James Cook. In 1778, the First Fleet, commanded by Captain Arthur Phillip, arrived with a cargo of convicts and marines as guards. Free settlers quickly followed, and until the mid-1800s the colony exported wool, timber and other rural products. In 1851, gold was found near Bathurst; copper was discovered at Cobar in 1869; and in 1883, silver, lead and zinc deposits led to the establishment of Broken Hill in the far south-west. Today's Australians are aware of their history as never before. Though transportation of convicts to New South Wales ceased in 1840, and many former mining centres have become ghost towns, their stories are not forgotten. Convict-built structures are carefully preserved, and ghost towns have come to life again, re-creating the boom days or taking on new roles as centres of artistic activity. The history of the Aboriginal peoples, who were part of the continent for tens of thousands of years before others arrived, is also being recognised and cherished.

Restored steam trains wind through spectacular scenery and are popular with tourists and enthusiasts. The train above runs on the Zig Zag Railway in the Blue Mountains, NSW.

AUSTRALIAN CAPITAL TERRITORY

AUSTRALIAN CAPITAL TERRITORY

The Australian Capital Territory surrounds Canberra, Australia's national capital. Though it is the smallest State, it contains more buildings of national significance than anywhere else in Australia. First amongst these is Parliament House, opened in 1988 and visited by the public 364 days each year. Its popularity is equalled, if not surpassed, by that of the Australian War Memorial, which contains relics of every conflict in which Australian troops have taken part. The National Library, the High Court, the National Gallery and the National Science and Technology Centre (Questacon) all stand between Parliament House and Lake Burley Griffin, in the "Parliamentary Triangle" planned by Canberra's chief architect, Walter Burley Griffin. Other Canberra landmarks include the Telstra Tower on Black Mountain, the Captain Cook Memorial Water Jet and the Carillon.

Opposite: A view across Parliament House and Lake Burley Griffin to Canberra city.

Above: The forecourt of Parliament House features a mosaic on an Aboriginal theme.

Canberra at night, the Australian War Memorial in the foreground. Across Lake Burley Griffin are (from left) the National Gallery, the High Court, Questacon and the National Library.

In a direct line with Anzac Avenue, the provisional Parliament House (1927–1988) stands in front of Parliament House. The Captain Cook Memorial Jet is in the right middle ground.

VICTORIA

THE GARDEN STATE

Melbourne was settled in 1835, when the Aboriginal people who had lived along the Yarra River and the shores of Port Phillip Bay for thousands of years allowed John Batman and a group of settlers to found a village there. The following year, "Batmania" became Melbourne, and in 1850 it was proclaimed capital of the new colony of Victoria. This was just in time to save revenues from the gold discovered near Ballarat and Bendigo in 1851 from the clutches of New South Wales. Melbourne became the financial capital of Australia, and stately buildings and beautiful gardens enriched the city. Wealth from gold founded many businesses, but wealth from the fine wools produced in the Western districts, the dairies of Gippsland, the wheat fields of the centre and west of the State and timber taken from the south-western forests has proved longer-lasting.

Victoria is rich in natural beauty as well. Travellers can enjoy many scenic features within a comparatively small area: the Great Ocean Road and the Grampians west of Melbourne, Wilsons Promontory to the east and the High Country of the Great Dividing Range are all prime favourites.

Opposite: The Yarra River flows through the heart of Melbourne, capital of Victoria.

Above: Brighton Beach, on Port Phillip Bay near Melbourne city, is noted for its bathing

Flinders Street Station, a triumph of Edwardian architecture, was completed in 1910. It is the hub of Melbourne's suburban rail lines and a well-known city landmark.

Fitzroy Gardens (left foreground) and the gardens of St Patrick's Cathedral and Victoria's Parliament House grace the eastern edge of Melbourne city.

GARDENS IN THE CITY

Melbourne is noted for its glorious public and private gardens and for its wide boulevards, bordered by stately trees. The Royal Botanic Gardens, around 35 ha in extent and near the city heart, echo the English landscaping tradition of the 1700s. Kings Domain surrounds Government House, the Shrine of Remembrance, Governor La Trobe's Cottage (1839) and the Sidney Myer Music Bowl. On the other side of the Yarra, Fitzroy Gardens is notable for its Conservatory and for Cook's Cottage (actually the residence of Captain James Cook's parents), brought from Yorkshire, England, in 1934. All these green refuges offer splendid floral displays, and are full of places to walk, talk with friends, enjoy family outings or just contemplate the beauty of the gardens.

The Conservatory in Fitzroy Gardens is one of the gems of a city where growing flowers is a passion and an artform.

West of Melbourne, the Great Ocean Road gives access to the coast and Port Campbell

National Park. The Twelve Apostles are limestone stacks carved from the cliffs by the sea.

WHERE SOUTHERN SEAS MEET THE LAND

Victoria's coastline has multiple personalities. Two of the most popular stretches of shoreline are completely different in conformation, aspect and atmosphere.

The Great Ocean Road, to the west of Melbourne, brings travellers to what was once called "the Shipwreck Coast" and today forms Port Campbell National Park. Here, islands and stacks have been sculpted as the relentless sea has undercut limestone cliffs, creating caves, then arches, then isolated pillars. Many vessels foundered on this rugged coastline, sometimes with considerable loss of life.

To Melbourne's west, Wilson's Promontory offers an extraordinary assortment of granite headlands, sandy beaches, flowering heathlands and rainforest gullies. "The Prom" is a prelude to the seemingly endless stretch of Ninety Mile Beach, which shelters the Gippsland Lakes from Bass Strait and the stormy Tasman Sea.

Wilsons Promontory National Park, 200 km south-east of Melbourne, offers spectacular views across granite headlands and blue waters to Bass Strait.

MAGIC MOUNTAINS

One branch of the Great Dividing Range dominates eastern Victoria, then dives under Bass Strait to reappear in Tasmania. It forms the High Country — snow-covered in winter — and is preserved as Alpine National Park, including Mount Bogong and, to its west, Mount Buffalo National Park.

The other keeps a low profile as it swings westwards and eventually rears into the four ranges that make up the Grampians. West of Melbourne, the Grampians stand in the midst of heath-covered plains, stretching 90 km north of the town of Dunkeld. The Wonderland circuit and Mt Victory Road take in the best-known lookouts, as well as Mackenzie Falls and rock formations such as the Pinnacle, the Balconies and Grand Canyon.

Mount Feathertop, in Alpine National Park, which encompasses the mountain peaks, alpine plains and wild river valleys of Victoria's High Country.

Mackenzie Falls, in the Grampians in western Victoria. These mountain ranges are steeper on the eastern slopes than on the west, and are the final extension of the Great Dividing Range.

Puffing Billy, an historic steam train, travels daily through the forests of the Dandenong Ranges between Belgrave and the Emerald Lakeside Park, just east of Melbourne.

VICTORIA GUARDS ITS HISTORY

Victoria gained its independence from New South Wales in 1850. Between 1851 and 1861, Victoria's population increased sevenfold as miners poured in from every part of the globe to mine the newly-discovered gold. As gold brought people, they formed a market for agricultural and industrial produce; the State prospered and transport, construction and manufacturing boomed. Today, re-creations of past places and ways are a big drawcard. Sovereign Hill and the Eureka Stockade re-enactment, which re-live the golden days of the 1850s, the Ned Kelly exhibits at Melbourne's Old Gaol and the historic steam engine Puffing Billy, Victoria's oldest steam locomotive, are prime favourites.

Sovereign Hill, at Ballarat, is a re-creation of a goldrush town of the 1850s. Cobb & Co were set up in 1853, carrying passengers and mail between Melbourne and the gold fields.

The Murray River forms much of the northern boundary of Victoria. Throughout the nineteenth century it was a commercial waterway. Today the paddlesteamers carry tourists.

A breeding colony of Australia's favourite marsupial, the Koala, flourishes at Healesville Sanctuary, 65 km from Melbourne.

OF KOALAS AND PENGUINS

Victoria is home to a wide variety of native creatures. Two of the most popular are the Koala and the Little Penguin, and both can easily be seen by visitors to Healesville Sanctuary and Phillip Island.

Healesville Sanctuary has been committed to caring for Australian wildlife for over 50 years and is especially well-known for breeding rare and endangered species such as the Platypus. Only a short drive west of Melbourne, Healesville displays many rare and not-so-rare species, including a fine colony of Koalas.

Another popular creature, the Little Penguin, is the main attraction at Phillip Island, where during the breeding season troupes of the endearing flightless birds emerge from the ocean at sunset and waddle up the beach to feed the chicks waiting in underground nests.

Little Penguins nest in many places along Victoria's coastline. The nightly "parade" of adults visiting their nests in the breeding season is a popular attraction at Phillip Island

TASMANIA

THE WILDERNESS STATE

Tasmania was cut off from the Australian mainland by rising sea levels around 12 000 years ago. Its Aboriginal history goes back tens of thousands of years — groups of Tasmania's indigenous people survived the great ice age of 18 000 years ago by sheltering in caves. The island's European history is much more recent and includes a period in the 1800s when it was a dreaded penal colony. Today, Tasmania's rugged west and south-west regions, scenic central plateau, fertile eastern farmland and glorious seacoast have earned the name "treasure island" for Australia's southernmost State.

Tasmania contains six World Heritage Areas and has been the scene of some of Australia's fiercest conservation battles. The Hartz Mountains, typical of the island's rugged uplands, were described by Sir Edmund Hillary, conqueror of Everest, as "some of the wildest and most spectacular scenery I have ever seen". The State's many glacier-shaped landscapes are in rugged contrast to areas where deep, rich soils allow the cultivation of crops, pastures and orchards.

Opposite: An aerial shot of Hobart, the Derwent River and the Tasman Bridge.

Above: The wild coast of Southwest National Park.

Hobart's harbourside Salamanca Place, where old warehouses now harbour artist's studios and craft workshops, is the scene of renowned weekend markets.

HOBART'S INSTITUTIONS

Standing on the shores of the Derwent River estuary, at the foot of majestic Mount Wellington, Hobart is a beautiful city in a splendid location. For many years it was a roaring seaport for sealers and whalers, and today the city's waterfront is still a focus of activity. Day to day there is a constant passage of pleasure craft, fishing vessels and cargo ships. At New Year Constitution Dock is deck-to-deck with ocean-going survivors of the Sydney to Hobart Yacht Race, and in February the Royal Hobart Regatta overwhelms Sullivans Cove. There are plenty of historic places in the city and suburbs — one of the most fascinating is Salamanca Place, its splendidly restored sandstone warehouses occupied by studios, galleries and select businesses; it is the site of popular weekend markets.

Sullivans Cove, in the Derwent River estuary, gives access to Constitution Dock and Victoria Dock, where yachts berth after completing the annual Sydney to Hobart Yacht Race.

LEGACIES OF A COLONIAL PAST

In 1642, Abel Tasman named a newly discovered island off the southern coast of New Holland "Van Diemen's Land", after the then Governor-General of the Dutch East India Company. In 1803, in order to forestall French interests thought to have an eye on the area's rich sealing and whaling trade, the British Government sent marines, convicts and settlers to claim the island. Transportation of convicts stopped in 1853, but a harsh prison established at Port Arthur, on the Tasman Peninsula was closed only in 1877.

Tasmania's lowlands have a temperate climate and rich soils, so that plants difficult to grow elsewhere in Australia often flourish there. Homesick settlers planted trees and flowers familiar to them, and Tasmanian gardens often strongly resemble those in "the old country".

The ruins of Port Arthur penal settlement, on the Tasman Peninsula. Established to punish re-offenders, Port Arthur was a much-feared place of suffering for its inmates.

Tasmania's temperate climate allows the cultivation of various European plants. One is lavender, which curves across the rich red soil in long swathes of amethyst blossoms.

Tasmania's east coast is warmer and less stormy than its western counterpart. Wineglass Bay, in Freycinet National Park, is one of the island's loveliest stretches of silver sand.

THE WILDERNESS CONFLICT

In Tasmania, the problems of industrial needs for raw materials versus the preservation of wilderness are continually raised. The island has magnificent forests, which in the past have supplied huge amounts of lumber for various purposes, including woodchipping. Where not protected by national park status, these forests are still being logged. They may be replaced by fast-growing "working forests", but these will be cut down well before they mature. Tasmania also has deposits of minerals whose extraction has caused environmental damage, and rivers which various agencies have, sometimes successfully, attempted to dam to create hydro-electric power. The island has seen some notable battles fought between conservation and development. So far, each side has some wins and some losses. Goodwill, co-operation and a realisation of the long-term effects of drastic environmental alteration will be required to balance the scales into the twenty-first century.

The Tasmanian Devil is Australia's largest remaining carnivorous marsupial. It is harmless to humans, feeding on easily-caught small creatures and even road kills.

Russell Falls, in Mount Field National Park, tumbles for 40 m over ledges and is a feature of one of Tasmania's most admired beauty spots.

SOUTH AUSTRALIA

THE FESTIVAL STATE

South Australia's capital, Adelaide, is set in the fertile and well-watered south-eastern corner of the State. It is a beautiful and spacious city, surrounded by parklands, and has a Festival Centre which allows theatrical and artistic productions to be presented in appropriate surroundings. Adelaide is home to a famous Festival of Arts and many other events; many towns and districts in South Australia have followed their capital's lead. They stage their own celebrations, from Hahndorf's German festivals to the York Peninsula's Kernewek Lowender, centred on Cornish themes, Port Lincoln's Tunarama, Tanunda's Oompah Festival and Mt Compass's Compass Cup, the Melbourne Cup of cow-racing.

The vineyards and orchards of the State's south-east contrast with the rugged starkness of the Flinders Ranges to the north, and the vast deserts which rule the entire north. In the south-west, headlands and beaches give way to the seemingly endless flatlands of the Nullarbor Plain, which looks down to the sea over spectacular limestone cliffs.

Opposite: An aerial of Adelaide over Torrens Lake and the Adelaide Festival Centre.

Above: In the arid north, a gnarled grass tree sends its flower spikes skywards.

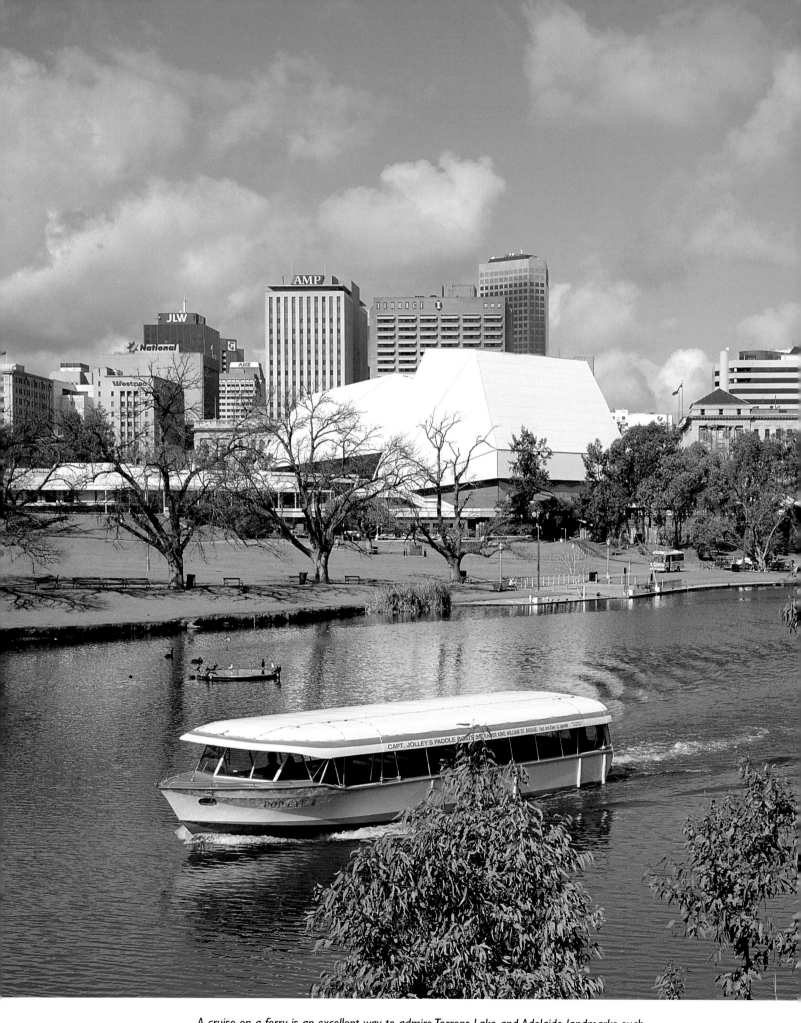

A cruise on a ferry is an excellent way to admire Torrens Lake and Adelaide landmarks such as Elder Park and the Adelaide Festival Centre.

ADELAIDE, A GRACIOUS CITY

Adelaide was founded in 1836 by free settlers. Thus, although it lacked the advantage of convict labour, it also escaped the many disadvantages of being a prison colony. Surveyor-General Colonel William Light drew up the plan for the city, on a simple grid pattern around five squares, surrounded by extensive parklands. His vision created a beautiful city. The Torrens River separates the city centre from North Adelaide, which is used for sport and recreation, with parks and sporting facilities lining its banks. The city itself contains many outstanding features. Classic buildings line North Terrace, which is also beautified by stately trees and a wealth of statues and monuments. Rundle Mall, Victoria Square, the Botanic Gardens, Adelaide Arcade, a variety of churches and cathedrals, the restaurants of Hindley Street and the East End Markets are also places to explore and enjoy.

Rundle Mall is a popular place to shop, eat, sit or stroll, enjoying the many sculptures with which the Mall is decorated.

A TREASURED HERITAGE

The lovely Adelaide Hills and the Barossa Valley have rich soils and a climate ideal for the cultivation of European fruits, especially grapes.

Hahndorf was settled in 1839 by German migrants searching for religious freedom. Today, Hahndorf proudly retains its German traditions and is a State Heritage town. The Barossa Valley, around 50 km north of Adelaide, was settled by other German groups in the 1840s. They cultivated their new land with care and today the Barossa is one of Australia's best-known wine-making regions, and the site of picturesque towns such as Bethany, Tanunda, Lyndoch, Nuriootpa and Angaston. Here the pages of history turn backwards for a glimpse of a past lifestyle, and nineteenth-century stone buildings house craft and art studios, as well as fascinating shops and galleries.

Hahndorf is known for its historic buildings, many of which house art and craft galleries.

The town of Tanunda, heart of the Barossa Valley, is surrounded by vineyards and wineries.

A peaceful spot on the Murray River, where it flows southwards to the sea through country made fertile with its waters.

HEART OF THE RIVERLAND

The Murray River travels more than 2500 km before it enters the sea at Lake Alexandrina, in South Australia's south-east. Entering South Australia from the Victorian border it flows westwards, supplying water for crops, orchards and vineyards in the area known as Riverland. At the town of Morgan, it turns south, to wind through the Murraylands, where wildlife and watersports, houseboats and heritage trails are key attractions for visitors. Finally it reaches Lake Alexandrina, near the wild Coorong, where a continuous sandbar separates coastal wetlands from the sea. This magnificent region is a paradise for birdlife and a mecca for nature lovers, campers and beach walkers.

Australian Pelicans are common along the course of the Murray, and are symbols of the great wild area called the Coorong, where the river finally enters the sea.

Four hundred and sixty kilometres north of Adelaide, the ancient rocks of the Flinders Ranges stretch for 400 km from Crystal Brook north to the edge of the Strzelecki Desert. The ranges are a continuing drawcard for artists and photographers, for from dawn to dusk sunlight paints the sheer cliffs, rocky outcrops and dramatic gorges in colours both subtle and strong. Spring rains bring mauve, red and yellow flowers to embroider the hill slopes and surrounding plains; rockpools and seasonal waterholes maintain wildlife such as the elusive Yellow-footed Rock-wallaby. The heart of the ranges is Wilpena Pound, a vast basin rimmed with jagged bluffs, whose Aboriginal name translates roughly as "bent fingers of a cupped hand". To the north, Gammon Ranges National Park is a rough and wild area, which looks farther north still to red sand dunes and salt lakes.

The rare Yellow-footed Rock-wallaby lives in the rocky mazes of the Flinders Ranges. It falls prey to foxes and eagles and must compete for the scarce grass with feral goats.

Rare rainfall has left a pool at the foot of a River Red Gum growing in a watercourse in the Flinders Ranges. The rocks of the ranges are up to 500 million years old.

These fantastic natural sculptures are called the Remarkable Rocks. They stand on the granite dome at Kirkpatrick Point, near Cape du Couedic, Kangaroo Island.

KANGAROO ISLAND

The third-largest island off Australia's shores, Kangaroo Island is 120 km south of Adelaide and easily reached by vehicular and passenger ferries or by air. In the early 1800s, the island was a base for sealers, whalers and escaped convicts, and relics of their presence can still be seen. It is also a wonderful place to see wildlife, since the fox, Dingo and rabbit never reached it. Echidnas, bandicoots and possums are plentiful, Koalas, penguins and kangaroos are easily seen, and the Australian Sea-lions of Seal Bay are a major attraction. Kangaroo Island is also beautiful: Remarkable Rocks at Cape du Couedic is its most famous scene. These strangely-shaped boulders were carved by wind and water, and have been coloured by brilliantly hued lichens. Other island sights include Kelly Hill caves and Admirals Arch; Murray Lagoon, in Cape Gantheaume Conservation Park is the home of flocks of water-loving birds.

Seal Bay Conservation Park is one of the best places to see rare Australian Sea-lions, such as this female and her pup, at close quarters.

WESTERN AUSTRALIA

STATE OF EXCITEMENT

Western Australia is so large and contains so much variety of landscape that selecting symbols to stand for the whole State is not easy. Perth and its guardian, the Swan River, are obvious icons. After that, there is almost too much to choose from.

The south-west and the southern coastline are characterised by rugged granite formations and tall trees; the Goldfields and Wheatbelt by plainlands studded with rocky tors such as Wave Rock and by drought-resistant desert eucalypts. North of Perth are the coastal columns of the Pinnacles, the dramatic sandstones of the Murchison River, the stunning coastline which posed such dangers to Dutch vessels centuries ago, and Shark Bay, with its dolphins and dugongs. The Hamersley Ranges stand stark among the spinifex and ghost gums, their gorges sheltering blue-green pools, their very substance rich in iron ores. Northwards again, past Ningaloo Marine Park, is Australia's final frontier, the mighty Kimberley Division, with its Boab trees, limestone ranges, impenetrable coastal wilderness, diamonds and pearls.

Opposite: Perth, seen at twilight across the calm Perth Water reach of the Swan River.

Above: The Bungle Bungles, Purnululu National Park, vast galleries of sculptured stone.

Nearly three-quarters of the population of Western Australia live in Perth and its port city, Fremantle. The climate is magnificent — cool, rainy winters, warm to hot dry summers and perfect weather in between. Perth spreads along a sandy coastal plain between the Darling Escarpment on the east and the Indian Ocean on the west. The city was founded in 1829, 19 km up the Swan River, where the waterway widens into Perth Water, while Fremantle was established where the Swan enters the ocean. Further upriver, the sandplains blend into fertile soil and the Swan River Valley is a place of flourishing vineyards.

The Swan River was once a busy commercial waterway. Today it is a playground, a sporting venue and a place where people come to fish, picnic, swim, mess about with boats and generally enjoy one of the most beautiful features of a truly beautiful city.

The Black Swan is the bird emblem of Western Australia. It is commonly seen on the Swan River and on the freshwater lakes of the coastal plain around Perth.

The Narrows Bridge spans the Swan River from the base of Mt Eliza to South Perth. Mid-left of this view is Kings Park, top left is Perth city and mid-right is Perth Water.

Western Australia is famous for its wildflowers. These include both the blossoms of fragile annual plants, and those of hardy perennials such as banksias, hakeas and eucalypts. Many grow well only in sandy or gravelly soils, but will flourish in gardens whose upkeep caters to their special needs. The State's annual wildflower display begins in the north-west in early spring, reaches the bushland and gardens in and around Perth in September and climaxes along the southern coastal heaths in summertime. After good late-winter rains, flowers paint both ground and trees in vivid colours.

The West has a multiplicity of insects, birds and mammals which interact with its plants and their flowers in a variety of ways, usually to the benefit of both partners. The plants offer nectar and pollen; the animals eat the nectar and transport the pollen to the next flower of the species visited.

The elegant Mangles' Kangaroo Paw, the State's floral emblem, is only one of a number of natural species and created varieties of a fantastic floral group.

Everlasting daisies, the paper-like blossoms of a hardy plant which flowers in great profusion in springtime after good winter rains.

ICONS OF THE MID-COAST

Between Perth and Shark Bay, the coast of Western Australia offers some extraordinary landforms. The town of Cervantes, some 250 km north from the capital, is the gateway to Nambung National Park, where the pillars known as the Pinnacles stand in ranks. They are composed of limestone set like concrete around the roots of vanished trees, then exposed by constant sea winds. A further 200 km north, where the Murchison River slows to reach the sea, Kalbarri National Park offers spectacular sandstone gorges and the remarkable Nature's Window frames a vista of the river and its surrounds. Finally, at least 860 km from Perth, Shark Bay's salt lagoons and red earth, give way to white shelly beaches where dolphins come to interact with people.

Nature's Window, a stone frame for a view of the Murchison River and the gorge it has sliced through the sandstones of Kalbarri National Park.

The Pinnacles, in Nambung National Park. Limestone pillars which formed around the remains of coastal plants, they range from mere stubs to formations five metres in height.

THE LEGENDARY KIMBERLEY

The Kimberley lies under the influence of the monsoons, which bring cyclonic rains during the Wet then retreat, leaving the land to dry out during winter. After the "build-up" (sometimes called the suicide season) of October and November, downpours transform the land from brown to green and set birds singing to advertise their breeding territories. In many Kimberley fastnesses, nature rules and the impact of humans seems minimal. It is easy to become entranced by the majesty of the ranges and by the spacious plains studded with boab trees and termite mounds. This is a country where crocodiles haunt waterways, where pearls are plucked from the sea and diamonds are mined from the land, where vast areas are protected from public access. The Aboriginal clans which have lived in the Kimberley for so long retain their cultures and are still a vital force in this remote area.

The Aboriginal peoples of the Kimberley painted figures from the Dreaming in caves and under rock overhangs. These works should be viewed with respect, for they are sacred.

Windjana Gorge, where the Aboriginal freedom fighter Jundamurra, also known as Pigeon,

made his base camp. The Pigeon Trail can be traced from here to Broome or Derby.

THE NORTHERN TERRITORY

NATURE TERRITORY

The Northern Territory can be viewed as two distinct regions. The Top End, the northernmost part of the Territory, is a land of great golden-grey sandstone escarpments over which waterfalls thunder during the Wet. Here, rivers loop lazily to the sea through vast wetlands teeming with waterbirds and crocodiles, in a land of woodlands, billabongs and an Aboriginal custodianship which has lasted some 60 000 years.

The transformation to the other famous region of the Territory, the Red Centre, begins southwards where the influence of the summer monsoon rains fades away. Grassy plains blend into stretches of red soil, scantily dressed in sparse bushes, and scattered with occasional white-trunked eucalypts where water exists underground. Good rain will bring this desert into bloom, but during dry seasons it lies quietly sunbaking, its wild creatures hiding during the hot days, emerging to live out their lives at night. In the Centre itself, the eroded stubs of gigantic mountains form the MacDonnell and other ranges, with their gorges guarding pools of cool water, and finally, in the south-west, the awesome rock formations known as Uluru and Kata-Tjuta.

Opposite: Darwin, capital of the Northern Territory. The Esplanade is in the foreground.

Above: A magnificent gum silhouetted against the MacDonnell Ranges of the Red Centre.

ULURU, THE ULTIMATE LANDMARK

Of all the Australian places awarded World Heritage listing, Uluru–Kata Tjuta National Park is surely the most instantly recognisable. The enormous monolith that is Uluru, and the stony domes of Kata Tjuta stand proudly above the desert plains, places of pilgrimage for outlanders and sacred trusts for the indigenous people of the Centre.

Uluru is 3.6 km long and stands 348 m above the plain. It may extend as much as three kilometres below the surface. Sunrise and sunset bring dramatic colour changes to "The Rock" and every visitor with a camera attempts to capture its special aura. The Anangu people are traditional guardians of Uluru and are willing to share knowledge of their culture with people who are interested. They do not approve of visitors climbing the monolith, and the number of tourists making the 1.6 km effort is diminishing.

The Red Centre flowers. Uluru is seen over a red dune system brilliant with new green growth and blossoms following substantial rainfall.

Uluru, an Australian icon recognised the world over. This massive sandstone rock extends far below the surface of the desert and is sacred to the Anangu indigenous people.

Litchfield National Park, about 100 km south of Darwin, contains some stunning cascades, which tumble into rainforest-surrounded pools. This is Florence Falls.

KAKADU AND LITCHFIELD

Kakadu National Park, 250 km east of Darwin, is a place every Australian should treasure. It is a world of dramatic cliffs, massive sandstone outliers, billabongs covered with lotus lilies, thundering waterfalls and rainforested gorges. Kakadu's sandstones are home to unequalled galleries of Aboriginal rock art, while its wetlands, replenished in every year's Wet by cascades falling from the Arnhem Land Escarpment, are alive with waterbirds.

Litchfield, only 115 km south of Darwin, has its own spectacular waterfalls, which tumble into pools surrounded by rainforest. Another feature of Litchfield is the remarkable area of weather-sculptured sandstone pills known as the Lost City.

Both Kakadu and Litchfield embody the spirit of Australia's Top End, where millions of years of earth history and tens of thousands of years of human history complement each other.

Twin Falls, in Kakadu National Park, pours from the heights of the Arnhem Land Escarpment into a deep rocky pool and thence to the coastal wetlands.

Crocodiles — those feared inhabitants of tropical waterways — are superbly adapted to their lives as aquatic predators. The Saltwater Crocodile is the only Australian animal which will attack and eat a human, and anyone looking at a large crocodile (and they can grow up to six metres long) must feel a shiver of apprehension. The Freshwater Crocodile, a much smaller reptile, eats fishes and other water life, and is harmless to humans unless molested by them.

A crocodile's upper body is protected by bony plates, its belly by tough, flattened scales. Eyes and nostrils are on the top of the head, allowing the owner to drift unobtrusively, watching for prey. The jaws gape widely and close with tremendous force, the 66 teeth crushing the victim's flesh, so that even if it escapes, shock and injury may still kill it. A flap of skin at the back of the throat allows a crocodile to open its mouth when submerged without taking in unwanted water.

This symbol of the north is a truly formidable creature.

The Saltwater Crocodile provokes a mixed reaction of fear and fascination. Armed and armoured to kill, a big "Saltie" may grow to 6 m and is a ruthless and efficient predator.

The rivers of the Top End of the Northern Territory run to the sea through wetlands fringed with pandanus trees. This tidal river country is ideal Saltwater Crocodile habitat.

AN ANCIENT, LIVING CULTURE

The coast of the Northern Territory is where indigenous people first made landfall on the Australian continent, more than 60 000 years ago. They developed a special relationship with the land they lived in, and evolved a range of cultural activities devoted to their society and the care of their country. Wherever the people lived they left records, often pictures engraved, stencilled, drawn or painted on rock. Many were created as part of the spiritual life of a group, others were records of happenings, teaching aids or were done in play. When Europeans arrived, there were about 126 tribal groups, speaking over 100 languages, living in the area now known as the Northern Territory, most in the Top End. Today, traditional culture and values are still respected and are being reclaimed by many groups. Indigenous people may be willing to share some of their values, customs and attitudes to their special places with those outsiders who show sincere interest.

Anbangbang Gallery at Nourlangie Rock, in Kakadu National Park, is a well-known example of Aboriginal art. For millennia these paintings were renewed by their guardians.

Ceremonies, whether serious or "playabout", are vital to Aboriginal culture. The preparations for the ceremony are just as important as the performance or ritual enacted.

QUEENSLAND

THE SUNSHINE STATE

To a Queenslander, it is almost unimaginable that anyone could want to live anywhere other than the Sunshine State. They are quietly satisfied to live in the State which contains such World Heritage marvels as the Great Barrier Reef, Australia's remaining wet tropical rainforest, and Fraser Island with its remarkable perched lakes and rainforest growing on sand. Added to them are coastal havens such as the Gold and Sunshine Coasts, the Whitsundays — the list could go on and on. And that is only the coast. Inland, there are the Great Dividing Ranges (with highland rainforest), the Darling Downs and Channel Country, the fossils of Riversleigh, the mysteries of Carnarvon Gorge, Lawn Hill Gorge and Cape York Peninsula.

Opposite: Brisbane, viewed over the Brisbane River and the Story Bridge.

Above: Lawn Hill Gorge, an oasis in the arid north-west.

The Pacific breakers roll in to Surfers Paradise, the most famous beach on Queensland's Gold Coast. South is Broadbeach, and west are the canal and river residential areas.

The dramatic cliffs of Indian Head on Fraser Island jut defiantly into the Pacific Ocean.

FRASER ISLAND AND THE SUNSHINE COAST

Sun-drenched resort towns are strung up the golden chain of Queensland's coastline like gems. The Sunshine Coast, just north of Brisbane, offers countless opportunities to savour sand, surf, sun and seafood that equal if not surpass the world's best. Just north, Great Sandy National Park includes forests, heaths and lakes. The park's great treasure is Fraser Island — World Heritage-listed and the world's largest sand island — a wonderland of beaches, sand dunes, rainforest, flowering heathlands and exquisite freshwater lakes.

The Noosa River winds to the sea past the town of Noosa, on the Sunshine Coast.

The Great Barrier Reef extends for around 2000 km north from Fraser Island to the Torres Strait. It may be divided into zones, the first from Bundaberg to the Whitsunday Islands, the second from the northerly Whitsundays to Hinchinbrook Island and the third northwards from Hinchinbrook. Each zone has its own access ports on the mainland and its own distinctive joys, but all offer an incredible experience which is becoming all too rare as the world's coral reefs succumb to pollution and climatic change.

Seeing the Great Barrier Reef for the first time from the air or a vessel is a stunning experience. Seeing it close-up, snorkelling or scuba diving, is amazing. It is a symphony in which colours, shapes and movement take the place of intricately assembled sounds, where life and death dramas take place in one of the earth's most glorious habitats.

Green Island, a coral cay 27 km from Cairns, is many people's first experience of the Reef.

Top: Cruise vessels leave Cairns marina for a day on the Great Barrier Reef.

Above: Townsville, on Cleveland Bay, is overlooked by the huge rock known as Castle Hill.

Tchupala Falls, one of the loveliest cascades in Wooroonooran National Park, a rainforested area around 30 km north of Innisfail.

TROPICAL RAINFOREST

Rainforests grow only where there is high and regular rainfall. Australia's rainforests existed 60 million years ago, when the continent was part of Gondwana, and were widespread across the continent for many millions of years. Climates changed, the continent grew drier, and fires, which favoured competing eucalypts and acacias, left the largest areas of rainforest on the eastern side of the crests of the Great Dividing Range. Logging and clearing for farmland has destroyed much of the rainforest which still stood in 1788, and it now exists only in isolated stands. However, these remnants are reservoirs of plants and animals seen nowhere else. It is an eerie feeling to stand amidst huge, buttressed rainforest trees and reflect that this cathedral-like forest, with its tapestries of mossy vines and creepers, once covered most of what we now regard as a supremely arid continent.

A Skyrail gondola, on its way from Caravonica Lakes, near Cairns, up the MacAlister Ranges to Kuranda. A trip on Skyrail gives a stunning view of the rainforest canopy.

Australia

Key
- National Park
- Marine Park
- Major road
- State boundary

Darwin
Yellow Water
Jim Jim Falls
ARNHEM LAND
Litchfield NP
Kakadu NP
Katherine River
Katherine
Nitmiluk NP

Wyndham
Kimberley
Purnululu NP
King Leopold Range

Broome

Port Hedland

Hamersley Range

Mt Augustus NP

WESTERN AUSTRALIA

NORTHERN TERITORY

Mt Isa

MacDonnell Ranges
West MacDonnell NP
Alice Springs

Uluru-Kata Tjuta NP

Simpson Desert NP
Simpson Desert

SOUTH AUSTRALIA

Channel Country

QUEENSLAND

Winton
Longreach
Jericho

Great Barrier Reef Marine Park

Low Isles
Daintree NP
Green Island
Wet Tropics World Heritage Area
Cairns

Townsville

Whitsunday Islands NP
Mackay
Great Barrier Reef Marine Park
Rockhampton
Lady Musgrave Island

Kalbarri NP

Pinnacles
Nambung NP
Swan River
Perth
Fremantle
Hyden
Wave Rock

Darling Range

Kalgoorlie

Nullarbor Plain

Flinders Ranges NP
Silverton
Broken Hill

Warrumbungle NP

NEW SOUTH WALES

Fraser Island
Cooloola NP
Sunshine Goast
Pumicestone Passage
Brisbane
Gold Coast
Lamington NP

Great Dividing Range

Blue Mountains NP
Sydney
Sydney Harbour
Belmore Falls
Morton NP

Porongorups NP
Stirling Range NP
Albany
Torndirrup NP

Barossa Valley
Tanunda
Adelaide

Flinders Chase NP
Kangaroo Island

VICTORIA

Grampians NP

Sovereign Hill
Twelve Apostles
Port Campbell NP
Port Phillip Bay
Otway Range

Ballarat
Melbourne

Alpine NP
Canberra
ACT
Kosciusko NP
Australian Alps
South Gippsland
Tarra-Bulga NP
Wilsons Promontory NP

TASMANIA

Launceston
Cradle Mtn-Lake St Clair NP
Mt Field NP
Hobart
South West NP

0   250   500
kilometres

120°E   130°E   140°E

−10°S
−20°S
−30°S
−40°S

31° 30'S
Lord Howe I.
Mutton Bird I.
Lord Howe Island
0   2
Kilometres
159° 05'E
Balls Pyramid

DISCOVERING THE ICONS

To discover icons, one first has to decide what icons actually are. The original reference was to a much-revered Russian religious painting, but the word has come to mean anything which inspires veneration as an extraordinary example of its kind.

Australia is a land of many faces. There is the Australia of the Aboriginal people, where every landscape is full of meaning. There is the Australia that the last two centuries have seen changed into a mosaic of cities and towns, farms and properties, bushland, wilderness and managed national parks. There is the Australia of koala, platypus and kangaroo, wonderful birds, remarkable reptiles and fantastic undersea life. All these Australias have iconic significance in some way to some people.

Discovering the essence of Australia — discovering the icons — is richly rewarding. The images in this book have been collected as those that epitomise this great land. They might serve as mementos of places and things that once seen are never forgotten, or as the inspiration to undertake the journey to see them with your own eyes. Or they might become your personal record of this land and its marvels, to cherish and revisit at will.

Kangaroos are Australia's totemic animals. Here, two male Eastern Grey Kangaroos strike an heraldic pose while sparring for dominance in their mob.

INDEX